Sell It Yourself

by

Craig M. Pattberg
Matthew W. Pattberg

Salt Lake City, Utah

Preface

You may need to toughen up just little bit. Some real estate agents are going to give you a hard time. If you follow my advice you can deflect most of it.

Don't let others scare you. This book contains all you ever wanted to know about selling your home privately but didn't know where to turn. It comes from years of involvement in the process as well as teaching other families how to do it.

Of course there are no guarantees in this book either written or implied. But selling your home on your own is not rocket science. Rocket science is much more predictable and has definite, concrete, mathematical rules that govern it. If you want to get to Mars, just follow the math. Quite the contrary is true when selling your home.

In selling your home you have to deal with humans. All bets are off on predictability with humans! Not only that, with a bunch of money at risk people may not act as they otherwise would.

This process can be intense, but you can get a good handle on it. If you are fair and reasonable and well prepared then you'll get by just fine, most of the time.

Where do I get off writing this book? And why should you bother to read it. First it's 'cheap' and second, where else can you find such an honest, open look at the selling privately process.

My college degree was in engineering (civil). But I spent the last 20 years of my working career as a real estate agent and investor (retired in 2016). I have purchased, fixed up and flipped over 20 homes. And at one time I owned and managed 13 rental properties.

So why am I writing this book? Because the time had come, someone had to. The increase in home values has made many people bitter about paying the high real estate commissions. So now it is worth it to try this on your own, at least for a month or so.

Table of Contents

Here are the majority of things that are important to know to save a big bucks!

Chapter Headings

1

What are the Odds

Approximately 8% of the total homes sold in 2015 were FSBOs (For Sale By Owners)[1]

This of course means that you might want to ask a few questions since the odds are not in your favor.

How can I improve the likelihood that my home will sell privately?

How can I set myself apart from the others on the market?

How can I make a deal when the time comes?

Good questions!

You can improve your chances to sell privately. It takes things like tenacity, chutzpah, exposure, exposure, exposure, etc. So never give up!

✓ People need to know about your home first.
✓ Once they know about your home, they need to be able to contact you to come see it.
✓ Then your home has to show well.
✓ Then you have to keep in contact with prospective buyers.
✓ Then you have to negotiate a deal.
✓ Then you need to close the deal.

2

A Few Rules of Thumb and Helpful Questions

You may see these elsewhere in the guidebook but here they are also for quick reference.

- If the flyers out in front of your home are being taken and you are not receiving calls from people wanting to see your home, then your price is mostly likely too high!
- If 5-7 people have come to see the inside of your home but no one makes an offer, then your price is most likely too high!

Are these folks good buyers (ask the following questions) ? :

- Do they have a home to sell (or a lease in a home or apartment)?
- When did they want to be in your new home by?

Are the buyers "pre-approved" yet (ask the following questions) ? :

- Have they seen a Loan Officer yet?
- Have they taken the Loan Officer their W2s (2 years), pay stubs and 3 months of bank statements?
- What is the name and phone number of their Loan Officer?

The first 4-6 weeks are critical. During this time frame the best educated buyers and the most likely ones to make an offer will come through. If you are priced right you should get offers early.

Fallacy: I can always come down on my price later!

You can, but you will most likely lose the best buyers. And it is very very hard to get any buyer to come back even if you had the foresight to make them sign in on your Guest Register <u>BEFORE</u> you took them through your home.

Some of this might make you feel a little uncomfortable but these things can separate you from the 92% of FSBOs that do not end up selling on their own.

These rules of thumb are designed to give you a 'feel' for what to expect and then be able to translate that into – what does it all mean.

We'll talk more about how to price your home properly later.

3

How to 'look' like a real estate agent

You are probably wondering why you might want to look like an agent. You will see in a moment.

As soon as you let it be known that your property is for sale, you will be greeted by an onslaught of real estate agents. Many agents that want to list your property.

They will have many reasons why they are more qualified to sell your home than you are. And they do know more than you do, but so what. You want to sell privately if possible. So we can use a distraction to start with.

You could have 30-50 agents contact you, depending where your property is located. Many will be respectful of what you are trying to do, but there will be some that will be condescending and some will be outright jerks.

You can avoid most of them by doing the following.

Anytime you advertise your property (flyers, sign, newspaper, Internet, etc), say that it is offered by "Owner/Agent". This will lead the real estate agents to think that you are 'one of them'. And if you were one of them it would mean that you do not need them. The effect of this is that they will not try to solicit your business.

So let's look at who 'you' are: you are the <u>owner</u> and you are acting as your own sales <u>agent</u>. So technically you are the owner/agent. That is not how real estate agents will think about. But calling yourself the owner/agent. So let them think that. It will save you a ton of time and aggravation dealing with them.

Now, if they start to contact you anyway, you can still deflect them by saying you have already chosen the agent that will list your property if you cannot get it sold yourself. And if you have anyone in your family that is a real estate agent, even if they do not live by you then you can tell them that you have an agent in the family. If they ask who it is, just say that is none of their business. Have them give you their card and tell them you will pass it along.

It's hard to believe, but they still may persist and be pushy. If this is the case just ask to leave or you will be reporting them to the local Board of Realtors. They will not want to be reported to the local Board.

I know this sounds a little extreme, but some real estate agents can be very pushy and condescending. But you do not have to put up with it.

4

Clean up, Fix up, Paint up!

I can't stress enough how important this is. It can help you get $1,000s more for your property.

Here are some easy things to do that will help the sale of your home go more quickly and for the best price. They take a minimum amount of time and money, and give great pay back.

Start by having a close friend that you know will be brutally honest with you do a "walk around" your home and property. Have them point out what they think are potential eye sores. Plead with them to be hard on you and your house. It will pay off.

The curb is the place to start. It is called "curb appeal" and it means that when someone drives up they want to get a good clean home to look at. It means no trike bikes on the lawn, no gutters hanging down. It means grass mowed and picked up, and the flower beds freshly weeded with new mulch on them.

Pay particular attention to the front door. Repair/replace the screen door and paint or stain the front door. Polish the door knob. Hose off the sidewalk. And don't just do these things the first day. Keep the sidewalks and other areas clean all the time and always have the lawn mowed on Friday before the weekend.

Sound like a hassle? Well it could save you $7,000 - $25,000 or more.

Once inside, clutter is the biggest thing to control. If you have little kids this is a constant concern. People that are coming through your home will have a very hard time visualizing how it will look as their home. They only see how it looks now. You are no longer the most important person in your home, the buyers are. And they need help in seeing themselves moving into your home. The less clutter the easier for them to see it as their home.

The bathroom and kitchen are two big culprits. Remove anything that is not nailed down. This means toothbrushes, razors, hair dryers. In the kitchen it means bread makers, coffee maker, salt & sugar, etc. Each item left out creates a feeling that the area is smaller than it is.

Also, take down any personal/family pictures. Replace them will anything that fits your decor. You do this so that they can picture 'themselves' in your home.

5

The Contract Paperwork!

It's a must! You just cannot get away from it. You have to sign something eventually to make it legal.

Remember this, "The one asking the questions is in control.". If you fill out the paperwork, the deal is slanted in your favor. Standard paperwork is not leaning in a particular direction, but the one who fills it out automatically makes it lean in their favor.

Don't let the buyer come to the party with the paperwork. And if they do come in with the paperwork, do not sign. Say you have to run it by your attorney first. If they came prepared, they have all the advantages. It is slanted in their favor.

If you have the contract paperwork and have practiced filling it out then you are miles ahead of the buyers. You will also know if you feel like it is beyond your capability. If it is beyond your capability then talk to an attorney or a title company. It's money well spent.

A contract can be written on a napkin, matchbook, legal pad, etc., etc. But you might want to use the paperwork that Realtors use. It is designed to minimize problems later. You can probably get a copy from a title company. Office supply stores have real estate sales contracts too. And of course the Internet is a great source.

Whichever contract you decide to use, practice filling it out at least 6 times, preferably 10 times. Practice makes close to perfect. Come up with different scenarios. Seriously, this is one of the most important parts of the transaction so don't skip over this part lightly. Take it serious and practice. You will be glad you did.

You will be very uncomfortable if someone else comes in with a contract in hand and expects you to sign it. Don't let that happen. Decide now that it is

YOUR contract that you use to seal the deal. Remember that everything is 'negotiable'. But the paperwork does not have to be.

Find a title company and go see them in advance. They will be very helpful. If attorneys have to be involved go talk to a few to see what they provide. They have great information for you. They can help demystify much of the "transfer of title" maze. You'll be glad you took the time to do this

When a deal comes in, have the earnest money check made out to the title company or attorney. It will make the buyers feel better about writing a check to a 3rd party and it takes you off the hook for any screw ups later.

Check out www.LawDepot.com for free real estate contracts. The nice part about it is that you can pick the state that the transaction is in. This site was still live and free as of 11/11/17. If they ever quit doing it for free, certainly someone else will start to offer this service. Just 'google' real estate purchase contract.

6

Pricing, Pricing, Pricing!

I used to have a long chapter to discuss pricing, but it was sugar coated and didn't get to the point quickly enough. Now I don't waste any time getting it done.

I have been teaching families how to sell their homes privately since 1995. My experience tells me that almost always the FSBO has overpriced the home.

The sad thing is that the first 4-6 weeks are the most productive and yet invariably the home will be overpriced during this crucial time. This is sad because the best time to get the best offer is early on. As time goes by the likelihood of getting the most money from the home is diminished.

I used to suggest that the price of the home not be published anywhere and then taught how to monitor incoming calls to gain feedback on the price. But this was hard for homeowners to implement.

So, instead of beating around the bush, let me reiterate the two rules of thumb I gave you earlier.

- If the flyers out in front of your home are being taken and you are not receiving calls from people wanting to see your home, then your price is mostly likely too high!
- If 5-7 people have come to see the inside of your home but no one makes an offer, then your price is most likely too high!

Pricing is where most FSBOs lose it. It is the hardest thing to do well and it will make your experience either pleasant or unpleasant.

Price your home to sell. It sounds appropriate doesn't it? You need to be at (or preferably below) "fair market value". People will not pay more than you home is worth (and you wouldn't either).

Most FSBOs will price their home too high thinking that they can always come down. But the greatest chance you have to sell your home comes in the first few weeks and if you miss that opportunity you can languish on the market for months. You see once someone has been through your home and felt that it was overpriced, it is very very hard to ever get them back!

Realtors, appraisers, mortgage brokers and others working in this field full time rarely can agree on the same price. If professionals cannot readily agree on a price then it should be obvious that the homeowner could have difficulty getting the price right.

A <u>mortgage broker</u> is not knowledgeable enough to help with pricing your home because their expertise is to find money for buyers. The <u>appraisal</u> is pretty good, but it can cost from $300-500 (or more depending on where the home is located). An appraiser's primary business is justifying prices for refinances (not setting prices for a home to sell). A <u>real estate agent</u> is qualified but might be biased because they want to **impress** you so that you will list your property with them. They might be inclined to promise more than they can deliver in order to get your business.

So whom do you use? I feel that you are capable of determining the price of your home. But you have to be careful because you are biased.

Here is the best way to accomplish this. Go walk though other homes that are on the market. Review "sold" data to see what others have been willing to pay. You can go see the homes on the market but you will have to rely on a Realtor or appraiser for the 'sold' data. I suggest you interview a few agents (2-3). Be up front and tell them you might want to try to sell your home yourself first. But you want to be prepared in case you need help so you are interviewing early. Be sure to get a list of homes that have recently sold from them. As a minimum get their thoughts on pricing.

When you go to see homes, you will need to develop a new mindset. Every time you go to a home to look at it, look for how it is <u>better than your home</u>. Actually make notes. Go to as many homes as you can that are similar to yours that are currently on the market. Try to stay very close to your home in size and area. By the time you have looked at 10 or more homes, you will have a feel for where your home should be priced. But you really have to work hard at not bragging to yourself about your home or you will miss the mark.

Once "fair market value" has been determined, which is what a willing buyer will pay, you can proceed. Realize that you cannot make your home be worth more than it is just by wanting it to be. Your home is worth what it's worth whether it is being sold privately or through the MLS (Multiple Listing Service) using a Realtor. That's it! Let me say that again because it is very important. Your home is only worth what it is worth no matter who is selling it (period)!

Professional Sign!

You stand to save thousands and thousands of dollars selling your home privately. Spend some of it on a good quality professional sign. A cheap sign looks cheap and will start you off on the wrong foot.

Use a professional to make your sign. They make YOU look professional.

Place it where it can most readily be seen. This might mean that you have two or even three signs. Just don't skimp on signs. Signs account for up to 50% of the phone calls that you will receive.

People will be driving neighbors looking for homes. They go where they want to live. So have a good sign. Don't underestimate the power of a sign.

If you live way off the main road, then place directional signs on the main street(s). Replace them often; they will only be a few dollars a piece. On the main street(s) put your address on the sign(s). Then have directional arrow signs to lead them in, much like you see done with garage sales signs. You will be amazed how much this will help.

Signs used to be the biggest contributor to activity with the highest potential to be the reason your home sold. But things have changed. Now the Internet is taking the lead for generating traffic.

8

Flyers & Handouts!

These are extremely helpful. Put them out by your sign in a tube or some protective container. People will take them. You will have to keep replacing them. Only put out 20-25 at a time and keep track of how many are taken. Remember that if flyers are being taken and no one is calling to see the inside, then you are most likely overpriced.

You need to have good basic facts about your home. You don't have to go into the fine details, just tell them how many bedrooms, how many baths, family room, storage, landscaping, sprinklers, swing sets, etc..

Put mortgage information on the flyer. Contact a mortgage professional and see if they will go in on the flyers with you – I'm sure they will. Show how much would be required as a down payment along with the current interest rate and monthly payments. Show what the qualifying income needs to be. No sense in having people coming through your home that cannot qualify for it.

Distribute flyers to friends, neighbors, relatives, co-workers, strangers, etc.. Don't think that the person you give the flyer to has to be looking for a home. Everybody knows somebody that is in the market for a home. So the people you give the flyers too will also know someone looking for a home.

Put flyers or post-its on cars in mall parking lots, in apartment complexes and put one in supermarkets with a color picture and "tear off" phone numbers. The more places you put the flyers the better. They can be very powerful since they will be circulated to people you would not normally get to meet.

It takes chutzpah! But it is well worth it.

9

Guest Register for Open House!

A guest register is a very important tool. Be sure to use one. Get name, phone and email.

Ask everyone to Please Sign In! Don't be pushy but don't let them just move on past the guest register. If they don't want to sign in then don't let them come through your home, simple as that. Just say it's a 'security thing'.

Seem harsh? Well who are these people anyway, have you ever met them before? Think about it, why would you let a stranger in now when you never have before! So just get them to sign in, it doesn't totally protect you but it will help.

You log in everyone that comes through your home. You keep it in a conspicuous spot by the front door. As people come in to preview your home you ask them to sign in.

Those who call in from the fact sheet or newspaper, log them in too. You capture their number on Caller ID, get their name when you call them back and put them on the guest register.

Why bother with all this anyway?

During the time you have your home on the market you may make changes. Typically that is from price reductions. If you know everyone that has shown an interest in your home you can call them and alert them to the changes.

You can also call to let them know if you are ready to list your property and will be raising the price. They just might want to come back and look again. Tell them that you only have two weeks to exclude them from the listing agreement. This will give it the sense of urgency that it might take to make one of the families go ahead and make an offer.

10

Newspaper Advertising!

I am not a big fan of this type of advertising. When I started in real estate is was the best way, now the Internet has taken over. But, if it is inexpensive it might be worth doing, especially in modest town or neighborhood publications.

The ad does not have to be elaborate at all. You don't have to spend a lot of money on ads either. Just put your home in the paper each Saturday and Sunday. Don't go for that five to seven day special, it's a waste of money.

In the ad(,)tell the city or area and the number of bedrooms and baths(,) along with one or two special items. Personally, I like to put the address also. This gets them to drive by. Driving by your home, they will see the fact sheet tube on your sign. They will stop and take a fact sheet and this will give them a lot of information on the house and the mortgage possibilities. They will now be able to see if the neighborhood is where they want to live. All these things help them to visualize if your home is the right one for them.

Change the 'special items' that you tell about your home each week. Be sure to put in the ad your phone number. In a subsequent chapter we'll talk about voice mail and caller ID. Both are extremely powerful tools to use. Because the more information you get out to the prospective buyers, the better off you will be.

11

Smart Phones

If you don't have one yet, you at least need a cell phone that has voice mail and caller ID.

On the voice mail, you give an in-depth description of your home. Also give them information about qualifying for a mortgage. The more information you give out the better. Include your address just in case they don't already have it.

Remember, they called you so it is quite appropriate to call them back. Be very casual on your return call. The most annoying thing about being a buyer is that "You can never get to speak to the owner!"

And here is an easy script to use when calling back someone who has called to hear about your home. "Hi this is John. You called and listened to a description on our home. Did you get all your questions answered? Would you like to come by for a private showing?"

Easy, huh?

As you get comfortable, you can ask them more questions to help you with your marketing.

P.S. I would dedicate a phone to selling your home. Do not answer the phone, let them listen to the voice message. Then see if they left a message and ultimately call them back to see if they want to come see your home.

P.P.S. I suggest you only show the home at certain times. For instance: Tuesday from 5-8pm, Thursday from 6-8 pm and Saturday between 12 – 4 pm. If you do not set limits, you will be at the mercy of these people. Buyers are used to not getting in at the drop of a hat, so don't let them.

12

Video Walk-Through

Nowadays video is the greatest way to get people engaged.

It may sound intimidating, talking about doing a video. The short answer is that it really is quite easy.

Any smart phone can do video. You don't need fancy equipment. It is the information, not the professionalism, that is important. The content is what people want and need. So give it to them.

A truism: you can screw up many things that are suggested in the guidebook and if the people like your home and the area, it will be hard to stop them from buying your home. The message here is that people don't care about you or your paperwork or your wording in an ad or the quality of your video. They care about the property and are more likely to be engaged when video is used.

So that said, get over any fears you might have and do this video.

Here is how I do all mine.

- straighten up your home
- don't write a script
- start outside
- at the curb, facing your house, take a 360 degree video
- from the curb, walk to and through your front door
- walk through the living room first, then dining room or great room,
- then the kitchen and bedrooms
- do the first floor first
- if you have a second level, do that next
- then do a lower level if you have one
- peek out to the backyard and then walk back through to the front door
- walk a few steps out the front door and look to the left and right
- then end the video

All during the video share a modest amount of information about what you are looking at. Do not go into great detail, if you do you will lose your audience. If you fumble along the way, start over.

I use Microsoft Movie Maker because it is free. Remember this is 'not' supposed to be overly professional. And the neat part about the program is that you can do the video in segments and just load the individual segments. Now if you don't like a segment you can just re-shoot the segment.

The 360 degree view of the front is one segment. The first floor can be a segment as can the upper and lower levels. If you cannot figure this part out, just get someone younger to help you – your kids, grand kids, nieces and nephews. If you have none of these available, hire a kid from local school.

Put the video on YouTube. Then send the link to everyone on earth – at least everyone on earth that you know. YouTube will take care of the rest for the planet.

Remember, 1) does not have to be perfect, 2) should be less than 3 minutes and 3) you cannot let fear stop you from doing this – it is too important.

13

The Internet

Although it is not necessary to have your own page, it may actually get you a better price. You will look more professional and people will not be as likely to give you 'low ball' offers.

There are several sites now available online to put your For Sale By Owner home. Some charge but others do not.

Right now, I like the following:

- GoDaddy has domain names and inexpensive, easy to use, websites. Make your domain name your address. (ie 123 South Main).
- Blogger.com – free and also a great one to use as your "home page" to display your home's pictures.
- Facebook (you can also create a page for your home and advertise for a modest fee).
- LinkedIn – more for business, but if you are already on it – then use it. Especially 'Groups'.
- YouTube – here is where you post videos of your home.
- Twitter – use it if you already have an account.
- Craigslist (some places around the country do well with this).

You can Google to find other sites that you pay for that can give you greater reach, like; www.forsalebyowner.com or www.fsbo.com.

The Internet is a very powerful tool. When we get an inquiry from out of state, they are very serious buyers so don't discount the power of the Internet.

Most older folks still love to hate the computer. If you are one of these, get your kids to help. They are so quick. You actually don't have to know much about computers. And usually your kids can show you how to get around online.

People from around the state and around the country can view your home online. They can get a description of the property as well as see where it is with a map and see what it looks like since your picture will be online too. It is truly amazing technology and will surely reshape how we do things in the future.

Don't be afraid of the Internet. Think of it as your tireless friend, ever present to show your home for you. And your computer is your link to the World!

14

Financing Options!

This is 'Greek' to most people. But it is so important that it would be a big mistake to ignore it. And you really should want to give the prospective buyer an idea of what it will take to purchase your home.

Put the following information on your voice mail, on the Internet and in the flyers you do:

Minimum down payment can be 'zero'
Minimum monthly payment
Interest rate used to calculate this
Income needed to qualify to purchase your home

Get help from the mortgage professional that is helping you with your flyers.

People buy homes like they buy cars. They want to know how much money they need to come up with initially (down payment) and then how much will it cost them monthly.

The affect of putting the financing information in each advertising place will work to screen out those that cannot possibly purchase your home. If with 3% down the minimum down payment is $4,500 and they only have $1,700 then there really is no reason for them to come look at your home. You may get fewer calls but they will tend to be better qualified. If you use a Realtor, they will take the opposite approach because all calls to them are leads for other properties too.

People actually need more than just the down payment. They also need closing costs (2-4% typically), a modest amount to start their escrow accounts (taxes and insurance) and most likely two months of reserves (2 months mortgage payments). So even zero down folks still need some money.

You can offer to contribute to the buyer's closing costs. It is a great tool to attract people. But all you really do is raise the price to them 1-2%.

Financing can make or break a deal. Don't treat this lightly. An informed buyer is a good buyer. You can minimize problems later if you take the time to do it right now.

Here are three non threatening questions to ask to see if the people are serious buyers:

1. Have you seen a Loan Officer yet?
2. Have you given them your W2s, pay stubs and bank statements?
3. What is your Loan Officer's name and phone number?

If they are serious buyers, these will not be a problem for them. If they are just "lookers" then they will feel slightly uncomfortable but will still answer your question.

Guerrilla Tools and Tactics

These tools & tactics have been demonstrated to be effective when used in a conscientiously applied program of verbal hi-jinks and regular professional dare!

✓ Send or deliver fact sheet flyers to 250 neighbors.

✓ Send or deliver fact sheet flyers to 100 business associates

✓ Send or deliver fact sheet flyers to 100 relatives

✓ Put fact sheet with color picture and "tear offs" at several local supermarkets. Find out the day of the week they clean off the bulletin board and replace every week.

✓ Put Post It Notes or fact sheets onto 1000 cars in supermarket ands mall parking lots

✓ Put Post It Notes or fact sheets onto 1000 cars in local apartment complexes

✓ Call everyone that shows up on Caller ID. Use the script and call everyone back.

✓ Use Guest Registers to sign people in. Call everyone that shows up on the Guest Registers.

✓ Have an "Open House" every Saturday and Sunday for the first 4-6 weeks. Alternate having it from 10am-2pm and 1pm-5pm. Have everyone sign in on the Guest Register. Open houses are not that well attended so be sure you have other things to do while waiting for someone to come through.

✓ Bake bread in the oven prior to your Open Houses (you can use Rhodes frozen bread it is really easy).

- ✓ Have soft music playing in the background.
- ✓ Turn all the lights on, ahead of time, when showing your home.
- ✓ Do not leave any valuables in the home, take them to relatives or put in the car.
- ✓ Do not follow people around telling them all the great things you have done to the home (write them down and hand them out).
- ✓ Never have your home be 'unavailable' for showings during your designated times.
- ✓ Try to 'hold your tongue', let them ask questions and do not talk too much.

Should I hold an Open House

Statistically your chances of selling your home at an Open House are not that good. But it is definitely one of the things that you can do as a FSBO. The primary reason should be to show friends, neighbors, co-workers & family. Buyers will normally come through open houses without an agent so if they need help with a loan qualification, just send them to the mortgage professional helping you.

It is best not to do an open house alone. Have your spouse, friend, neighbor or relative be your partner.

The good part is you get exposure and get to talk with people that might be interested in your home. The bad part is that you are vulnerable during and after the open house.

There was a great article in my local paper a couple of years ago that said, in essence, you have to be on the lookout for potential burglars.

About clutter, it is a good idea to not have any clutter whatsoever anywhere, so use this as an opportunity or excuse to remove all clutter. That includes calendars on the refrigerator, loose change on the dresser, all your jewelry, small electronics, credit cards, etc.. etc..

Be sure that everyone signs in the guest register and if you are really cautious you could have your partner jotting down license plate numbers. Have one of you go with each party that is going through the home. Don't bore them with small talk, but don't let them out of your sight either.

Take all your valuables and put them in a safety deposit box at the bank or in the trunk of your car.

17

<u>Can You Get Your Money Back?</u>

These are 'estimates' found on the Internet, regarding return on investment.

Add a room = 80-100% return

Remodel kitchen = 80-120% return

Remodel bathroom = 80-120% return

Add a deck = 45-75% return

Build a garage = 75-100% return

Add a swimming pool = 80-100% return

These are obviously estimates based on national numbers. They can help you to decide if you should consider doing some remodeling or fixing up.

For the most part you would only do these larger projects if you planned to stay in the home. But if you did them recently and now have to move then they can give you an idea whether you will be able to recoup the costs.

Property Critique Sheet

Use this to have a close friend, neighbor, or co-worker scrutinize your home. The tougher they will be, the better. You need 'other' eyes to do this. You are too close to it. Reward them for find 'faults'.

Outside:

Lawn & shrubs, trimmed & edged ___

Flower beds have been weeded and fresh mulch applied ____

All gates working/oiled hinges ____ Fencing in good repair ____

Decorative rocks or mulch replaced ____

Driveways & walkways sweep & clean ____

Mailbox in good condition ____ Outside lighting working ____

Garage door working & in good repair ____

Garage interior neat & clean (no clutter) ____

Garbage containers clean & lids on ____

No excess cars in driveways ____ Paint ____ Gutters ____

Screens ____ Front door clean/painted, no squeaks ____

Doorbell working ____ Clean windows ____

Inside:

No clutter _____ Walls bright & clean _____

Wallpaper in good repair _____ All lights working _____

Closets neat/well organized _____ Caulking in kitchen/bathroom _____
Leaky faucets _____

Switch plates clean _____ Clean or new carpets _____

Floors sparkling _____ No cobwebs/dust _____

All appliances working order _____ Clean oven _____ Clean refrigerator _____

Loose doors fixed _____ Sticky doors lubricated _____

Warped cabinets replaced _____

Excess furniture taken out _____ Air freshener in bath _____

Extremely neat/clean bathroom _____

19

<u>And little touches can help a lot.</u>

Fresh flowers, bread or cookies cooking, or popcorn

Live plants in living room and/or kitchen, throw pillows.

Soft music, no TV on .

Light fire in fireplace if possible.

A/C on early enough to cool home.

Keep pets outside (no exceptions).

Have all lights on including closets.

Have bedroom doors and bathroom open slightly.

Get light into home by opening shades, drapes, etc.

Never, never, never apologize for appearance.

Be courteous but do not use small talk.

They just want to look at your home.

<u>And consider the following:</u>

Be sure to be available to show your home.

Do not leave weekends unattended.

Fill your answering machine with information on your home.

Put possible financing options on your message.

Price is King so see every home that remotely resembles yours to get this part right.

Go through other homes, don't just pick up a flyer.

After you have seen 15+ homes you will begin to know what your home is worth.

Get a paid appraisal and offer it for free to potential buyers

GOOD LUCK!

And don't spend all the money you save in one place.

This book is not intended to be all-inclusive. And you cannot learn all there is to know just by reading it. But you will be leaps and bounds above other for sale by owners that have not read this.

There is no guarantee stated or implied regarding this book. Use it at your own risk.

98926860R00021

Made in the USA
Columbia, SC
03 July 2018